Fall Vibes

This book is dedicated to all
my basic witches, gorgeous ghouls
and pumpkin heads!
Have a beautiful season.

A Coloring Book By

Jennifer Amazon

Fall Vibes

A Coloring Book By

Jennifer Amazon

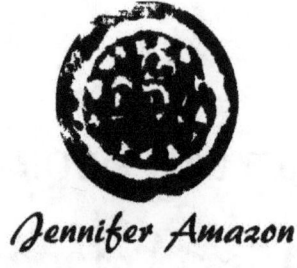

Jennifer Amazon

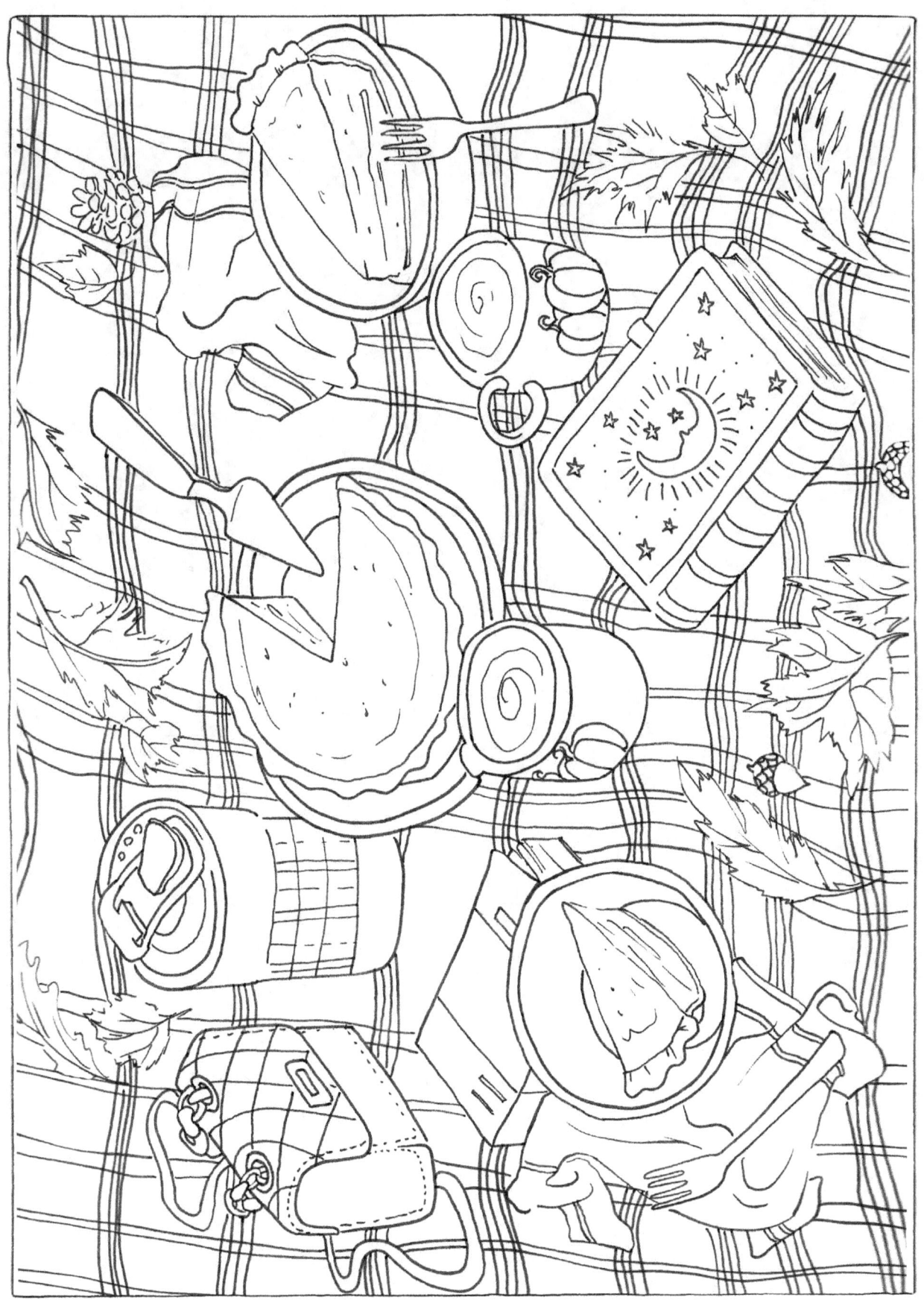

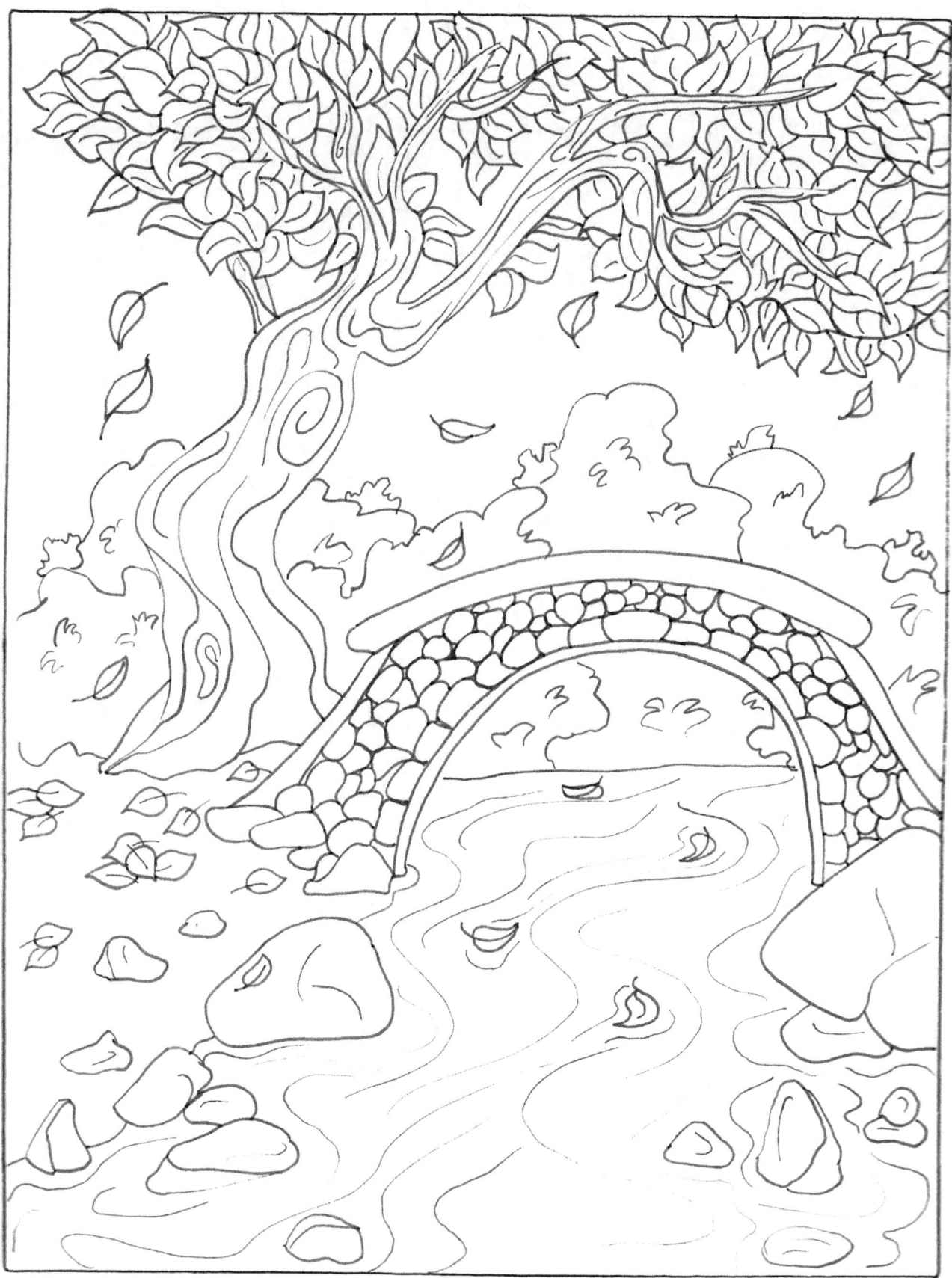

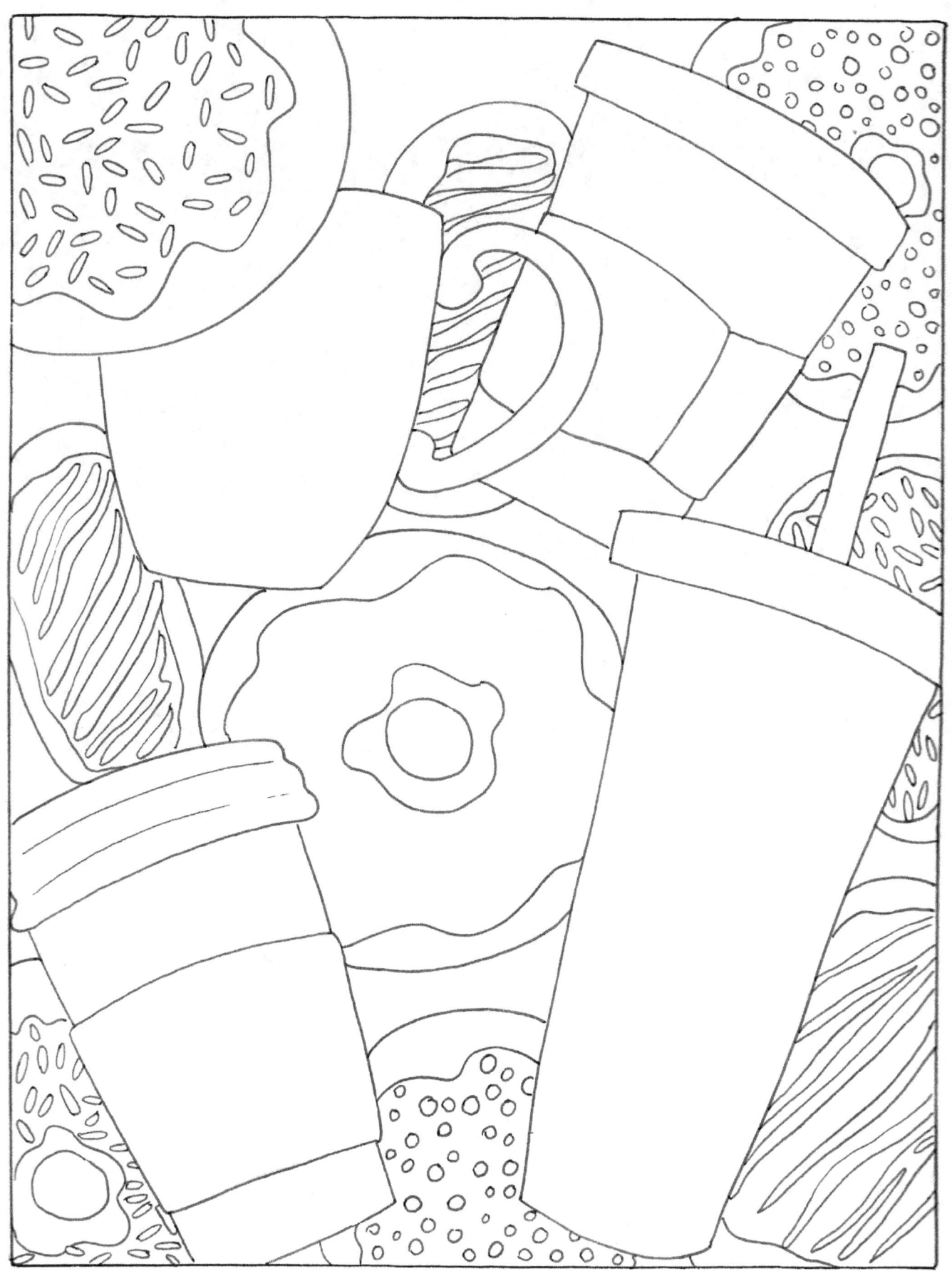

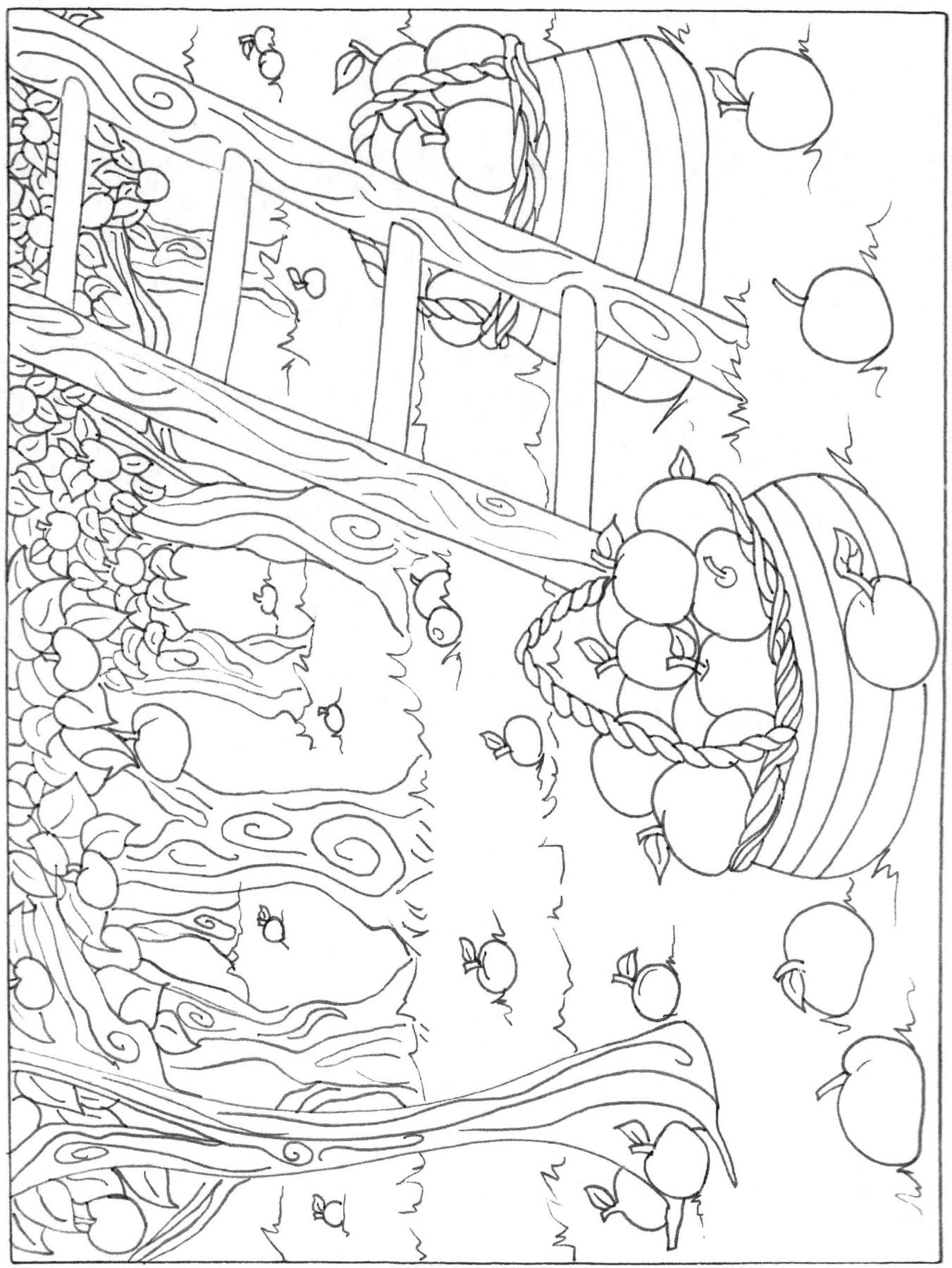

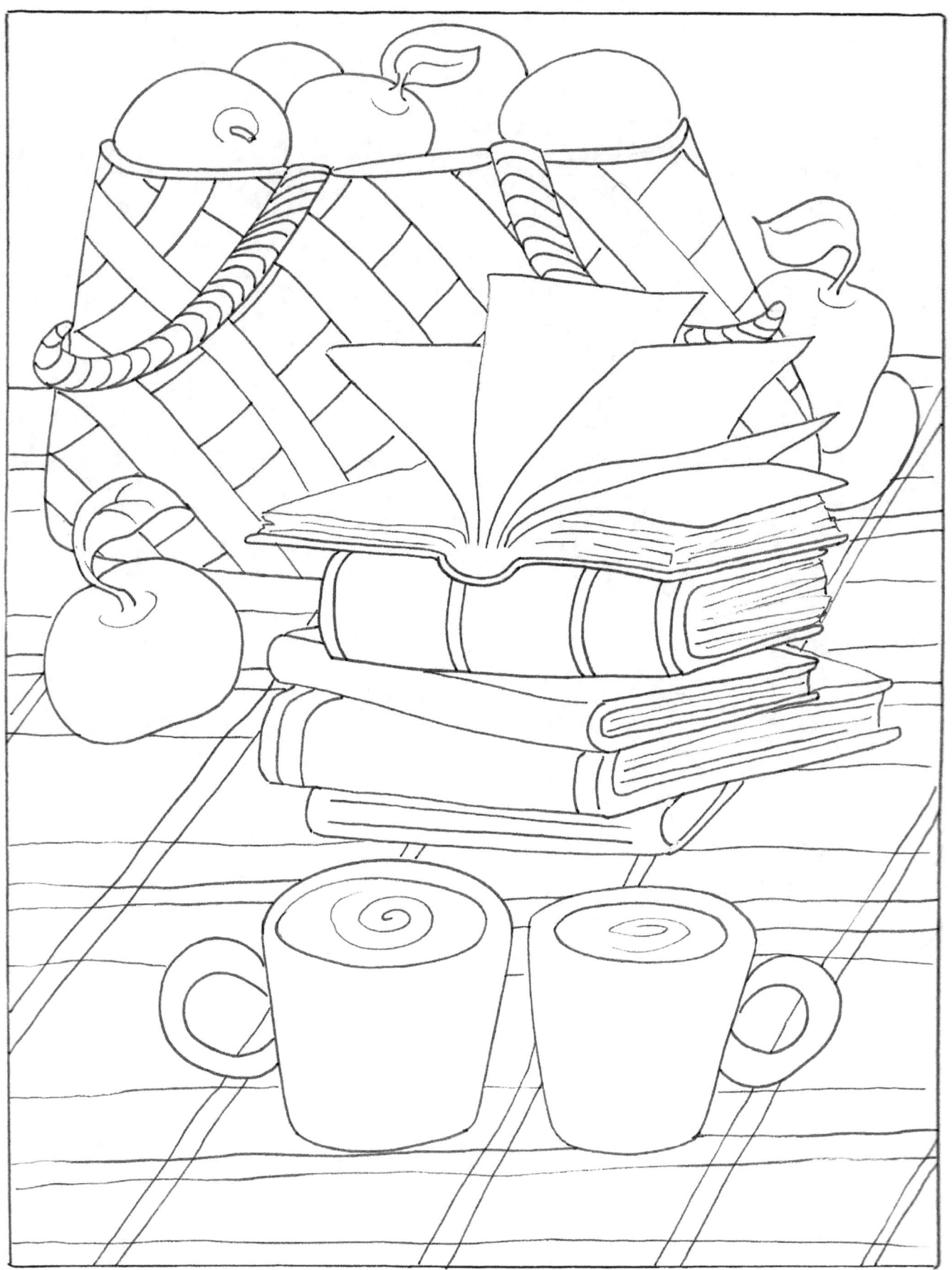

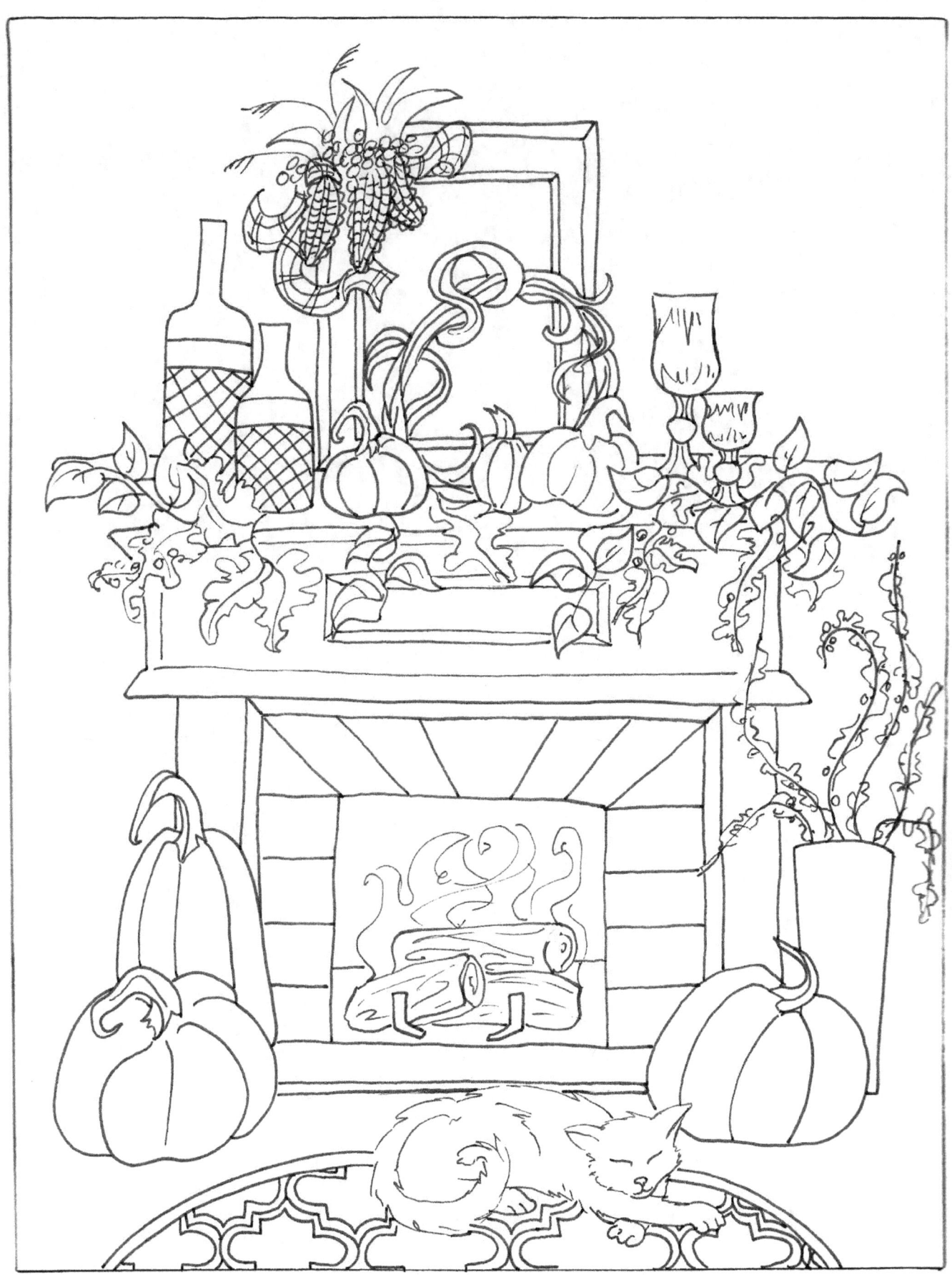

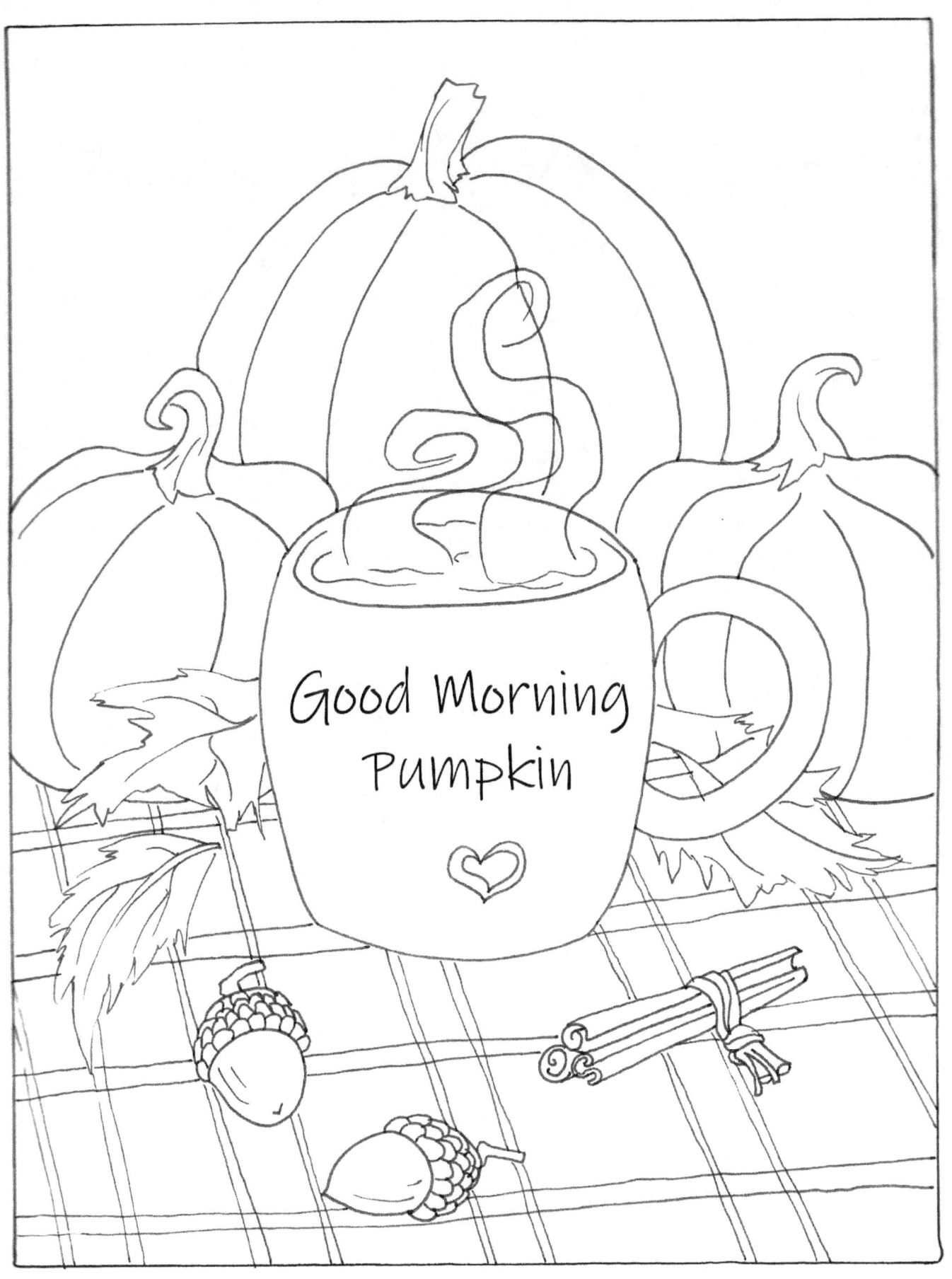

I love Fall most of all.

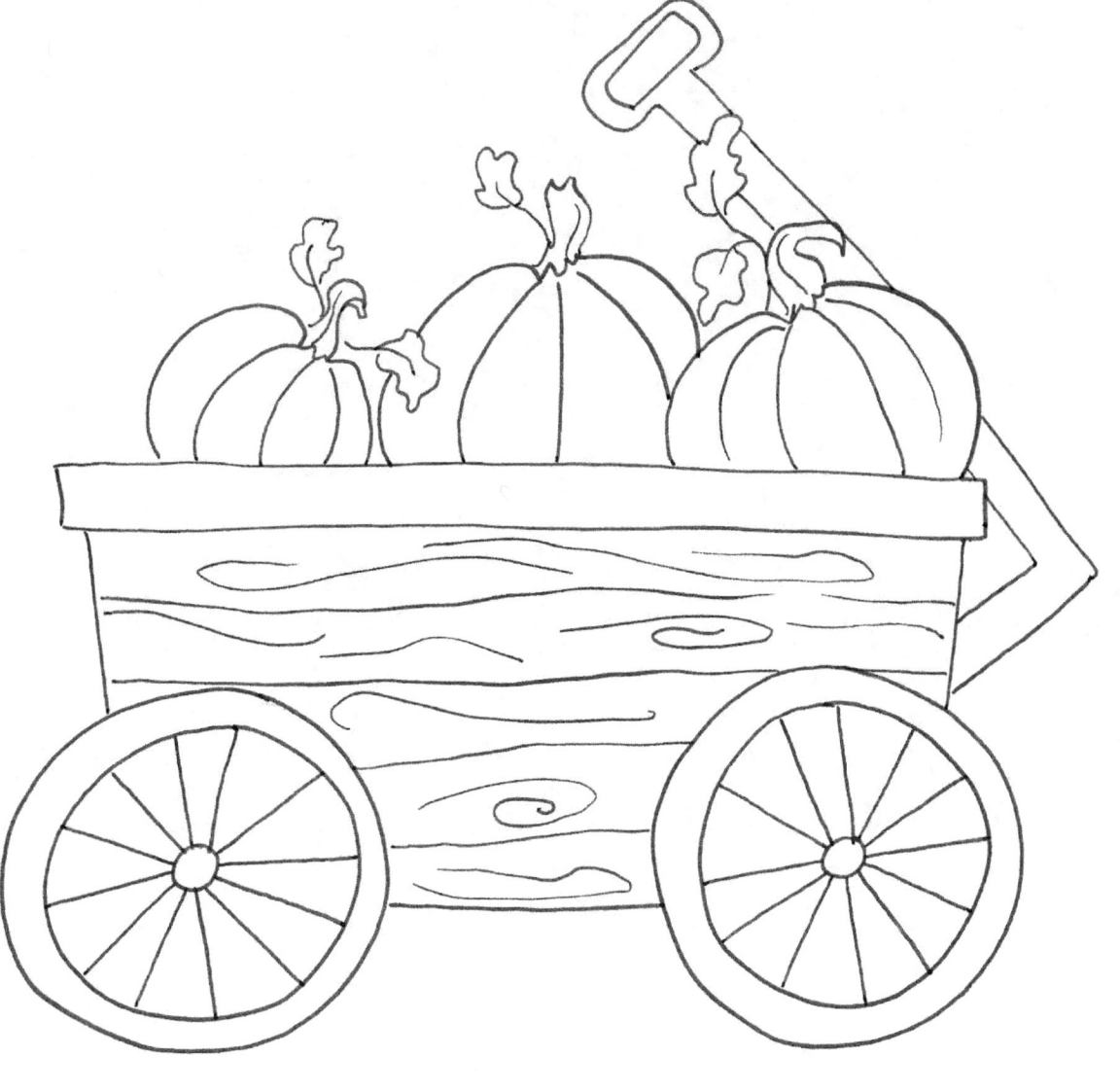

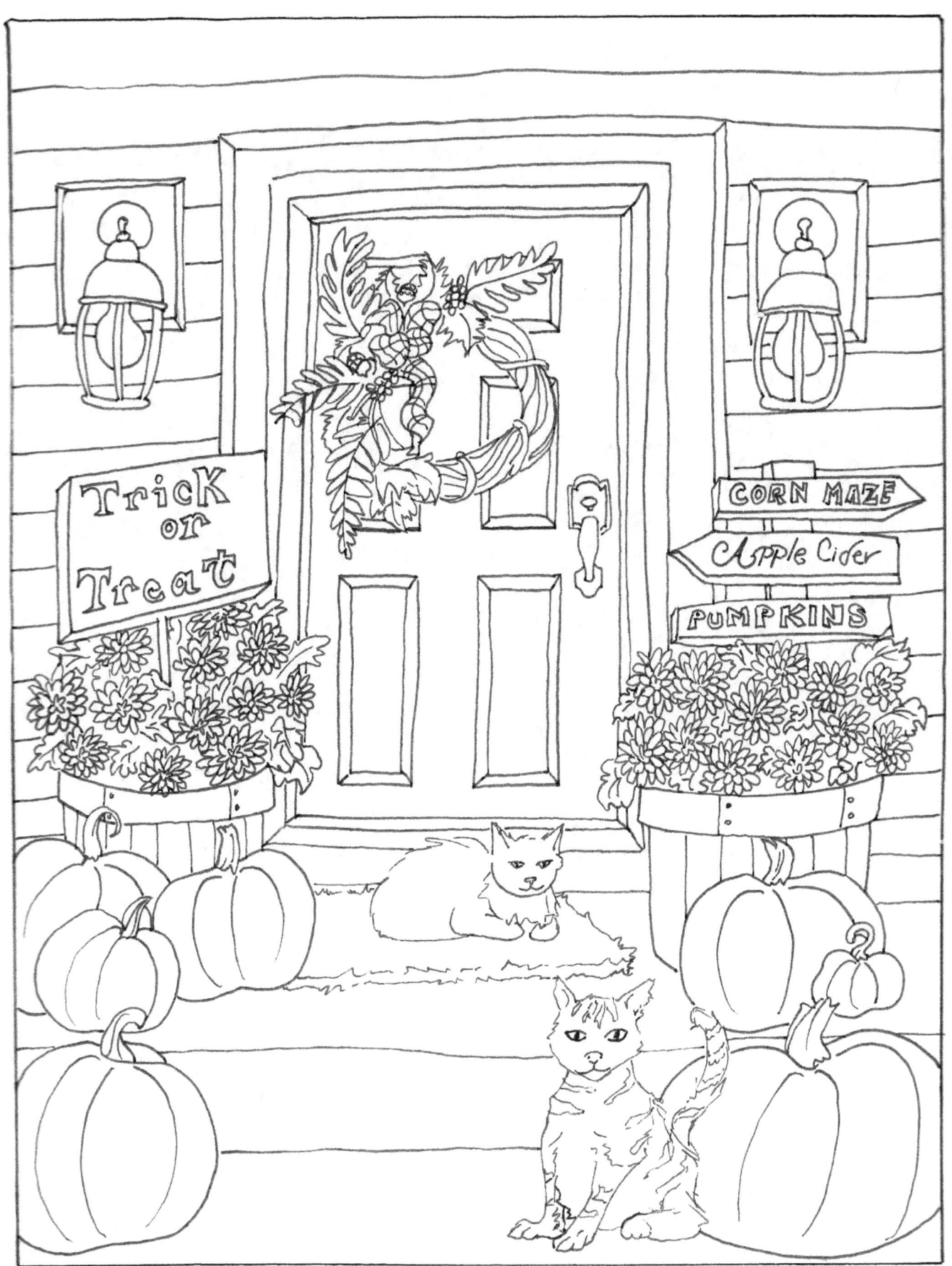

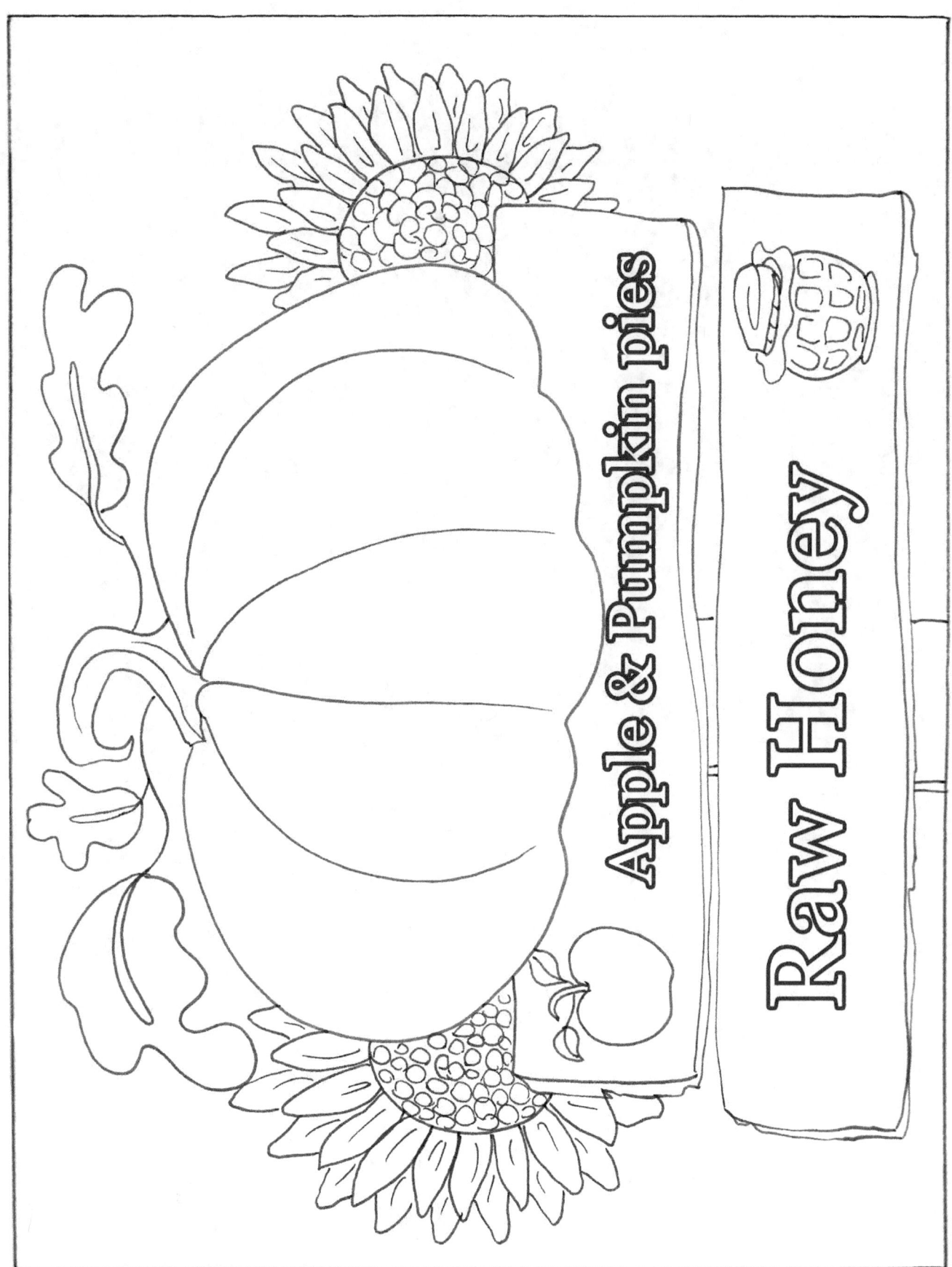

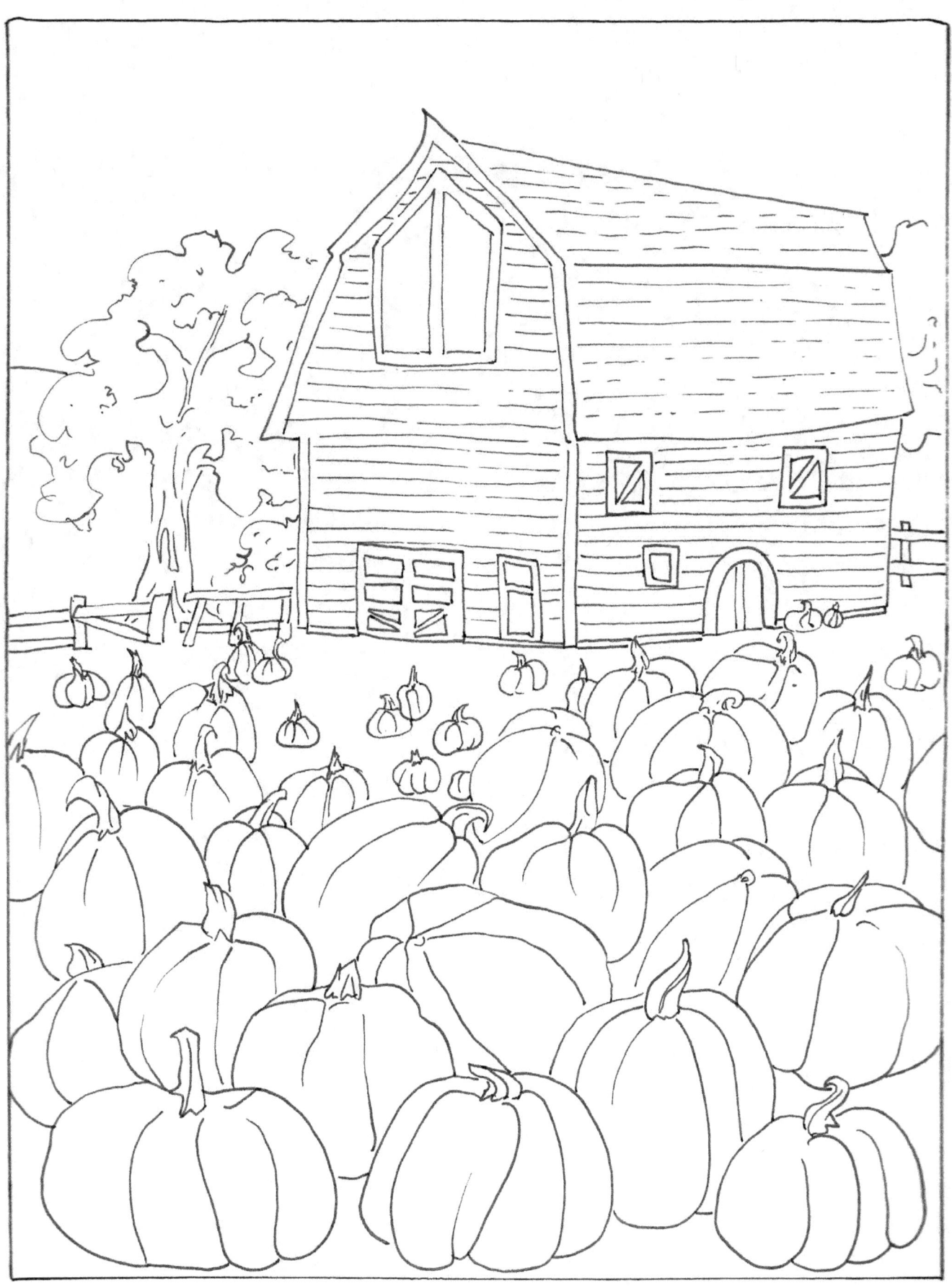

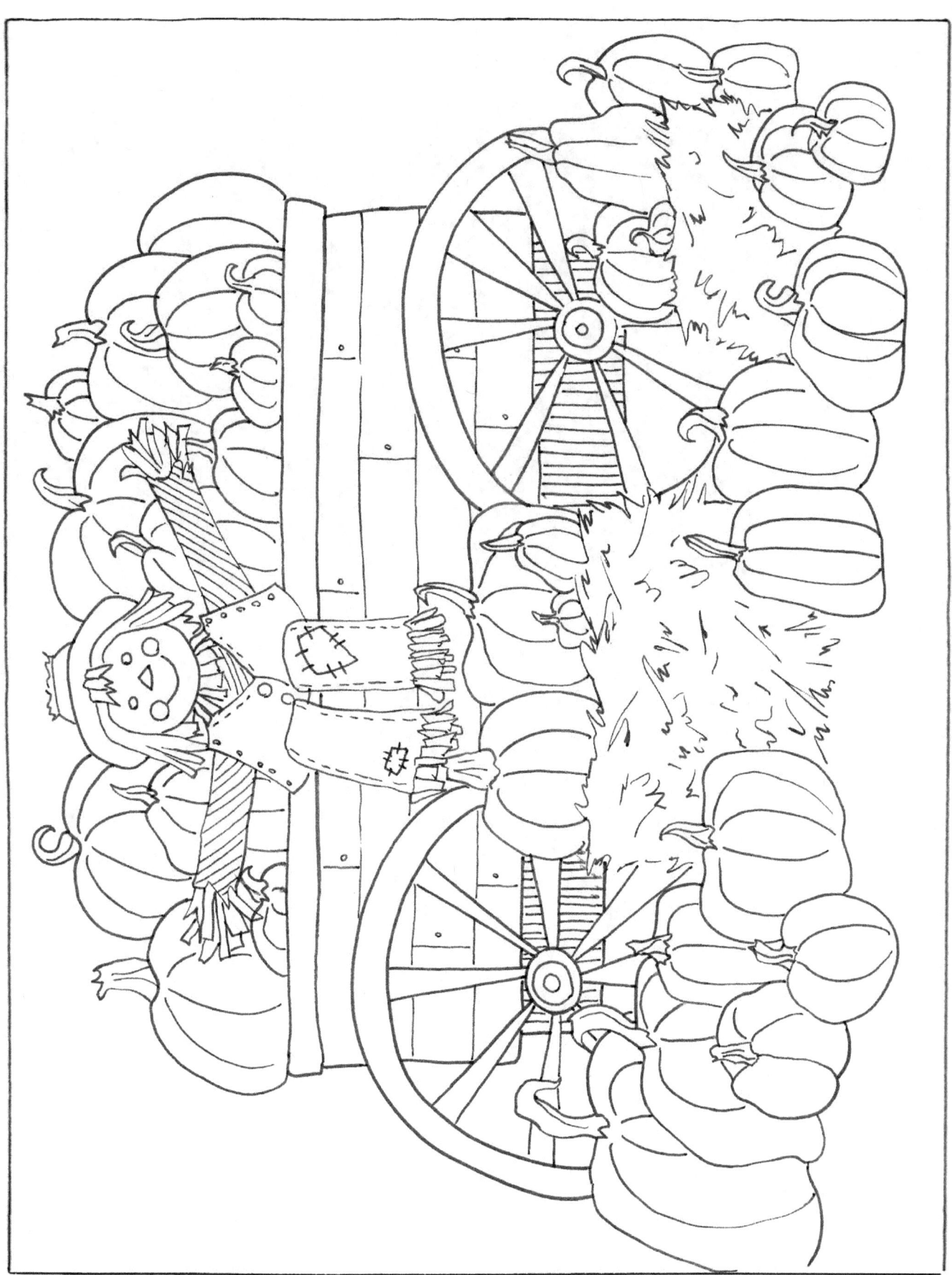

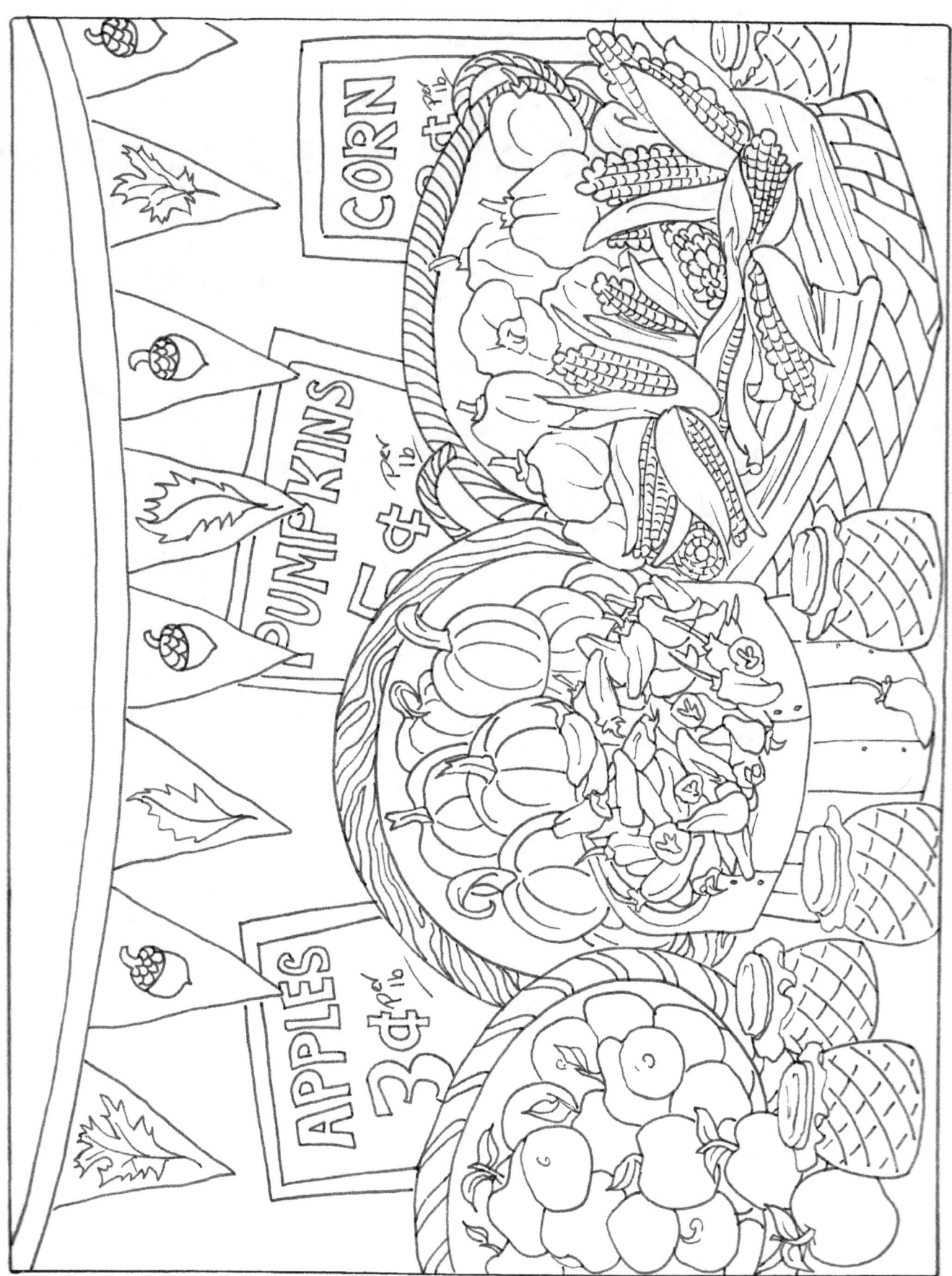

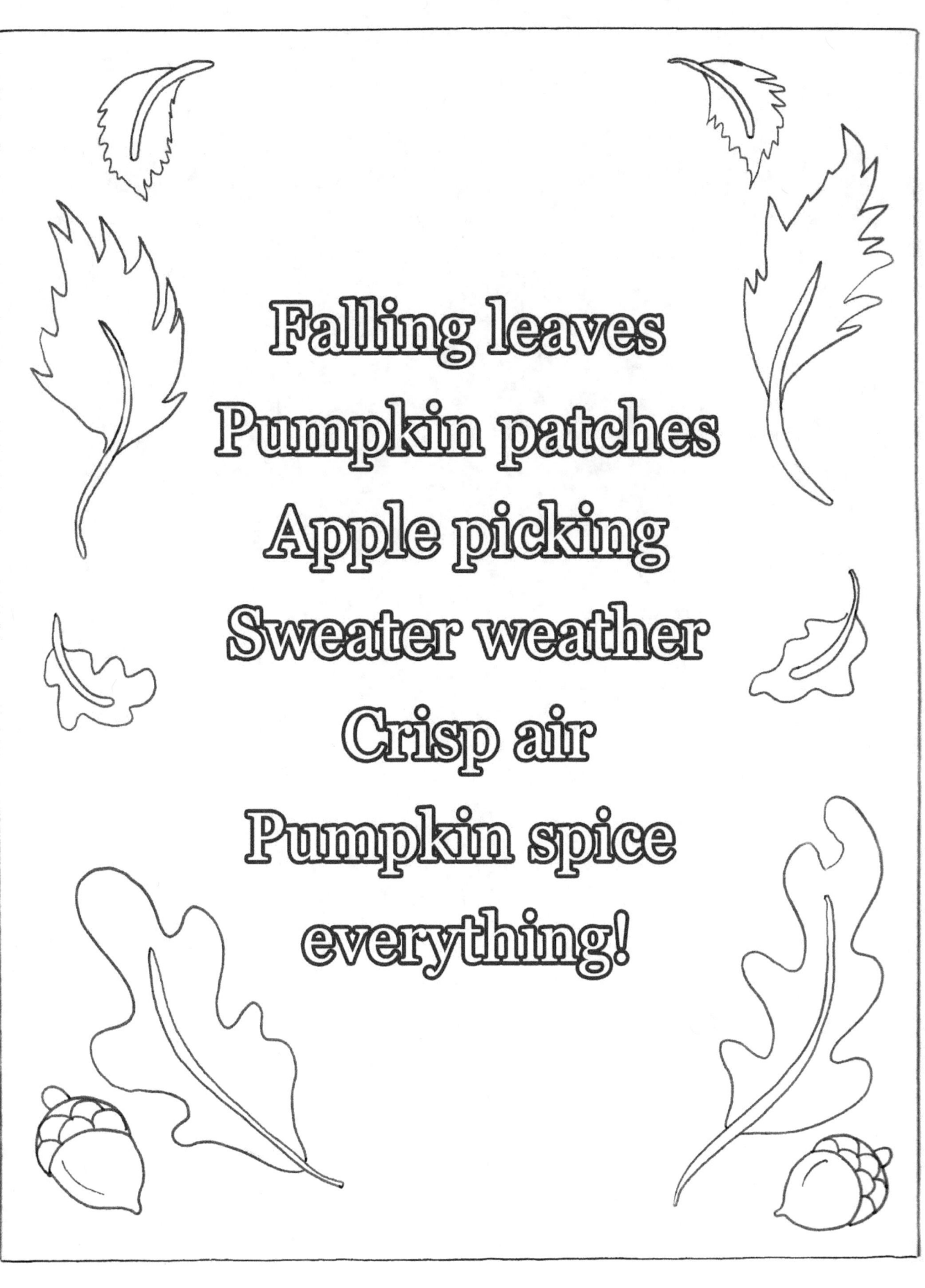

Falling leaves
Pumpkin patches
Apple picking
Sweater weather
Crisp air
Pumpkin spice
everything!

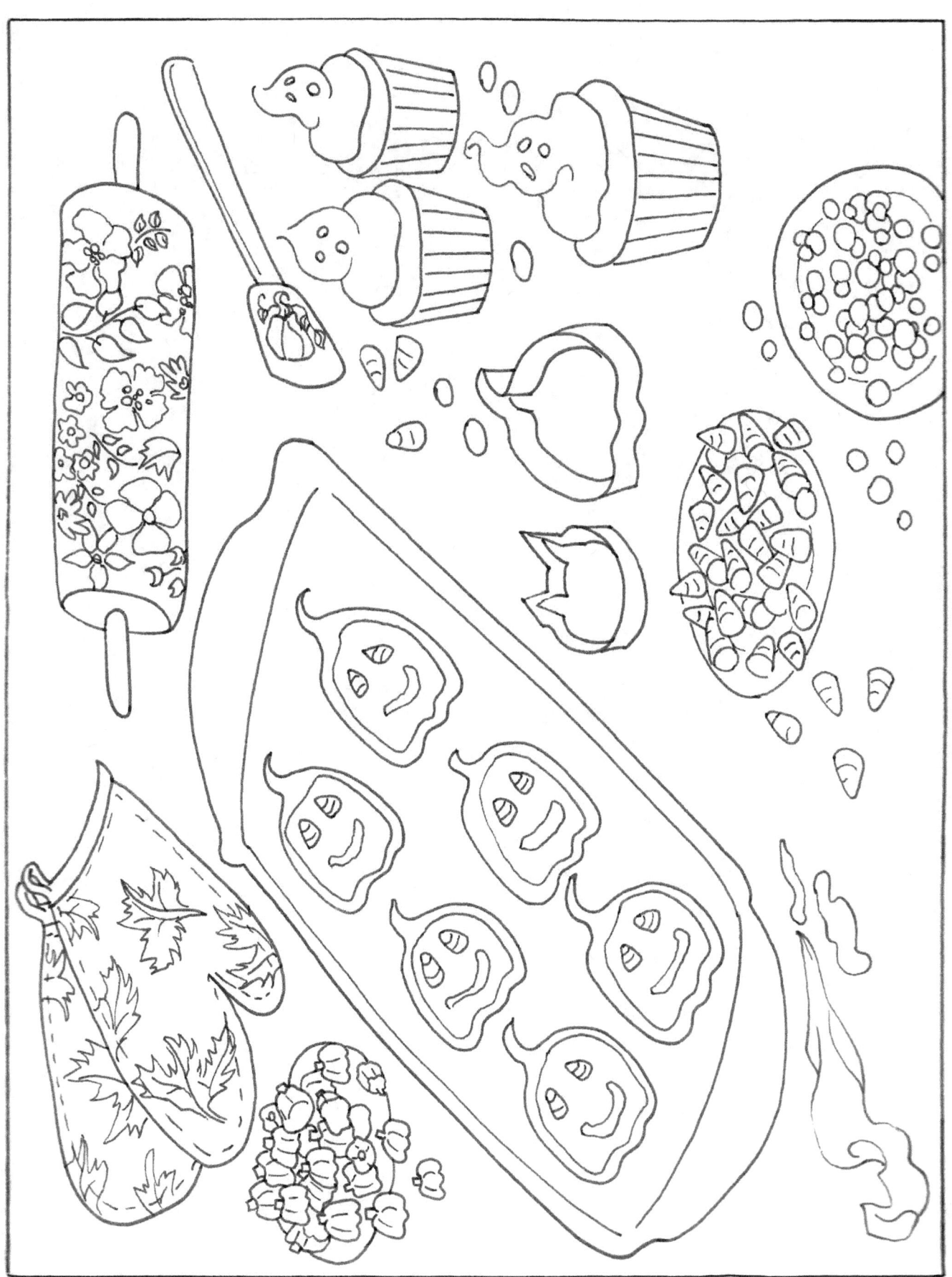

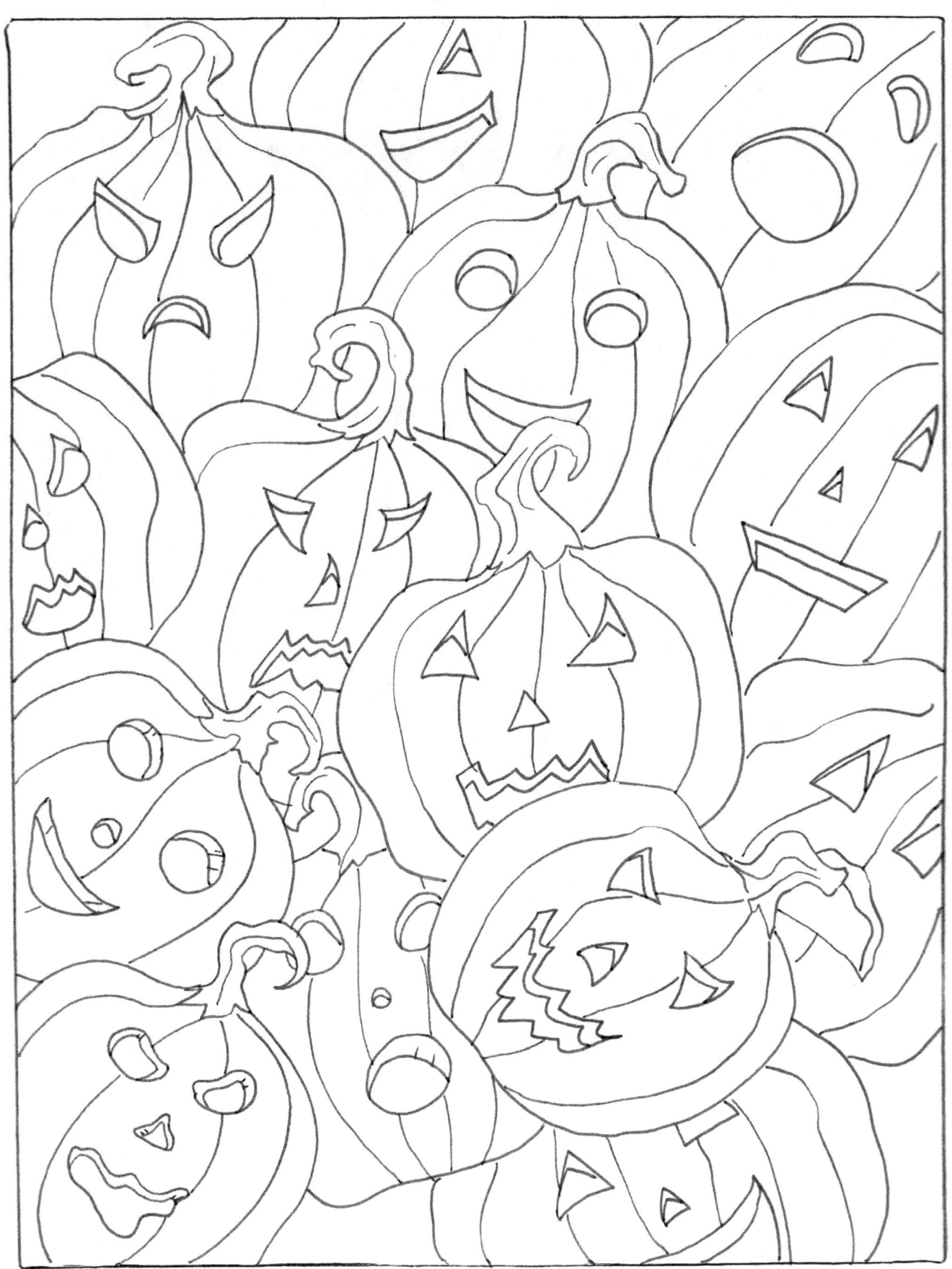

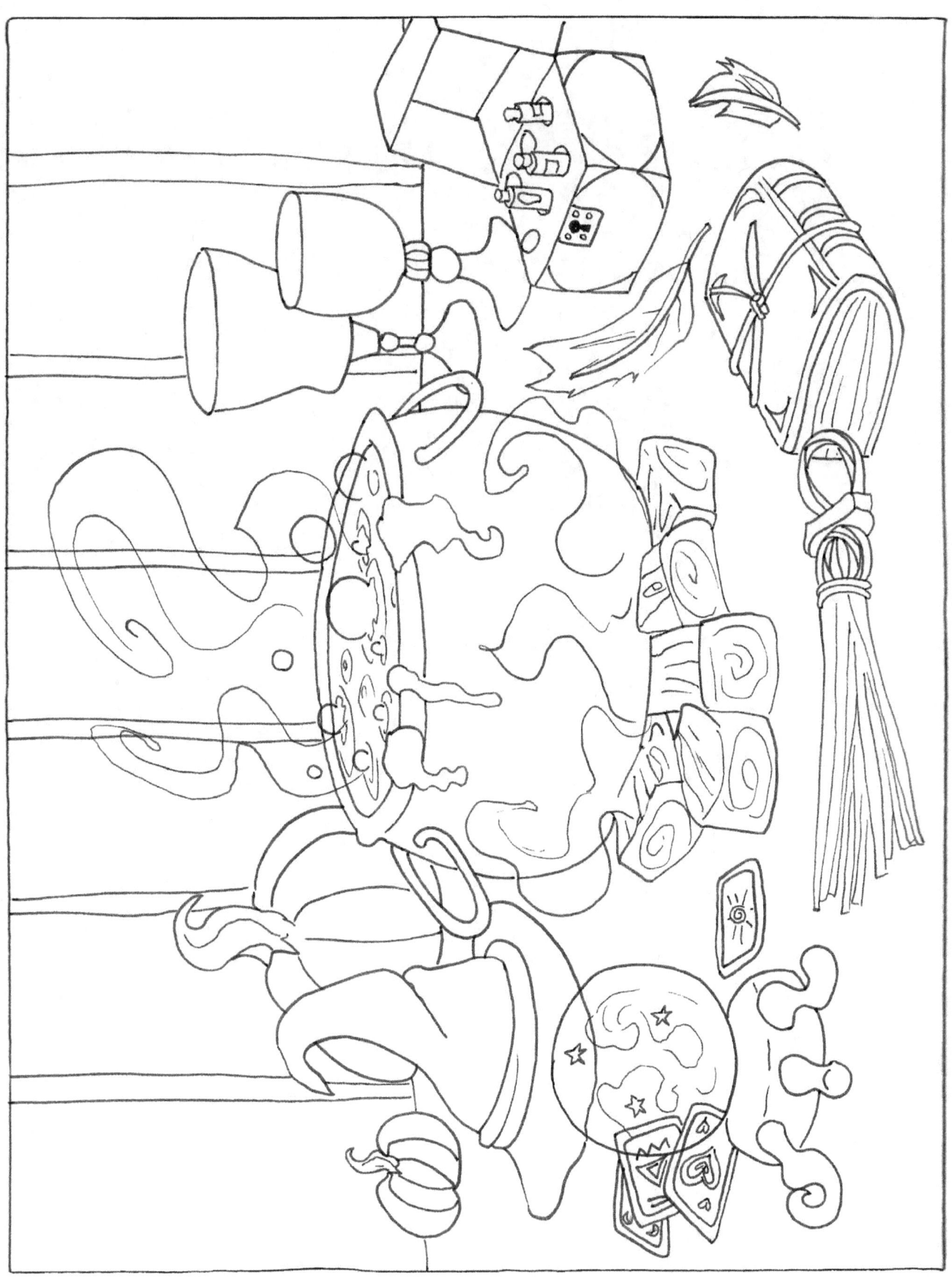

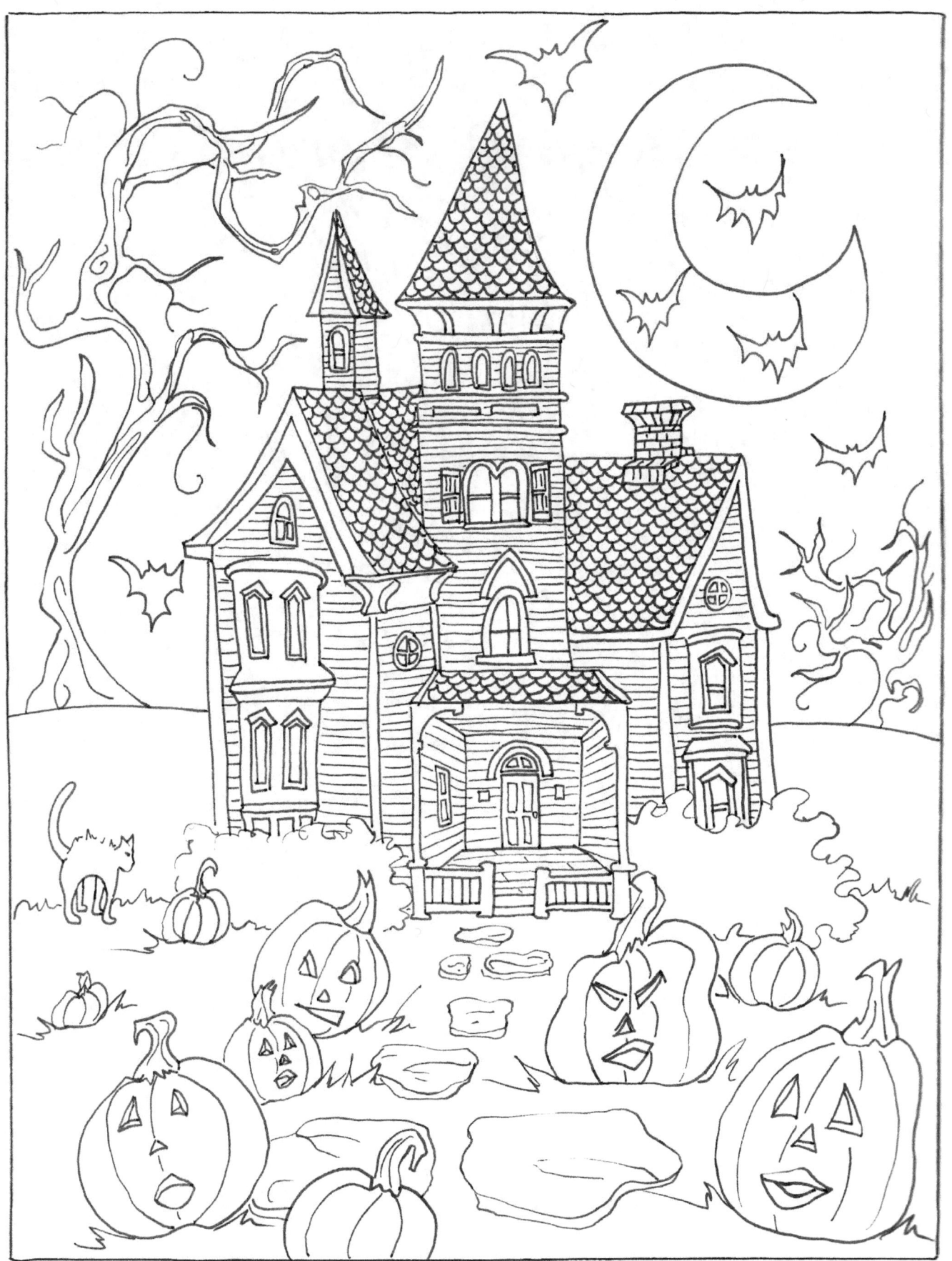

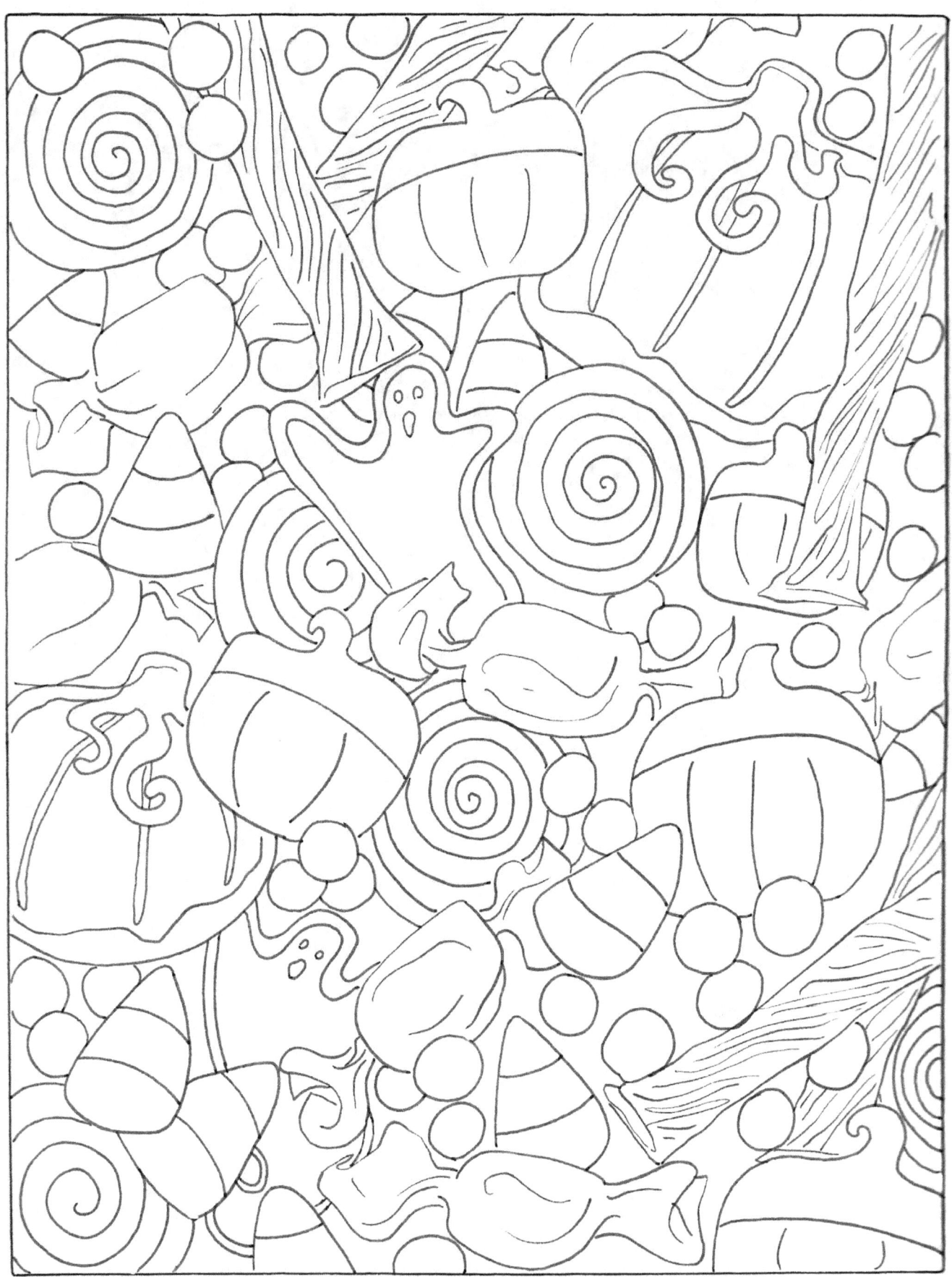

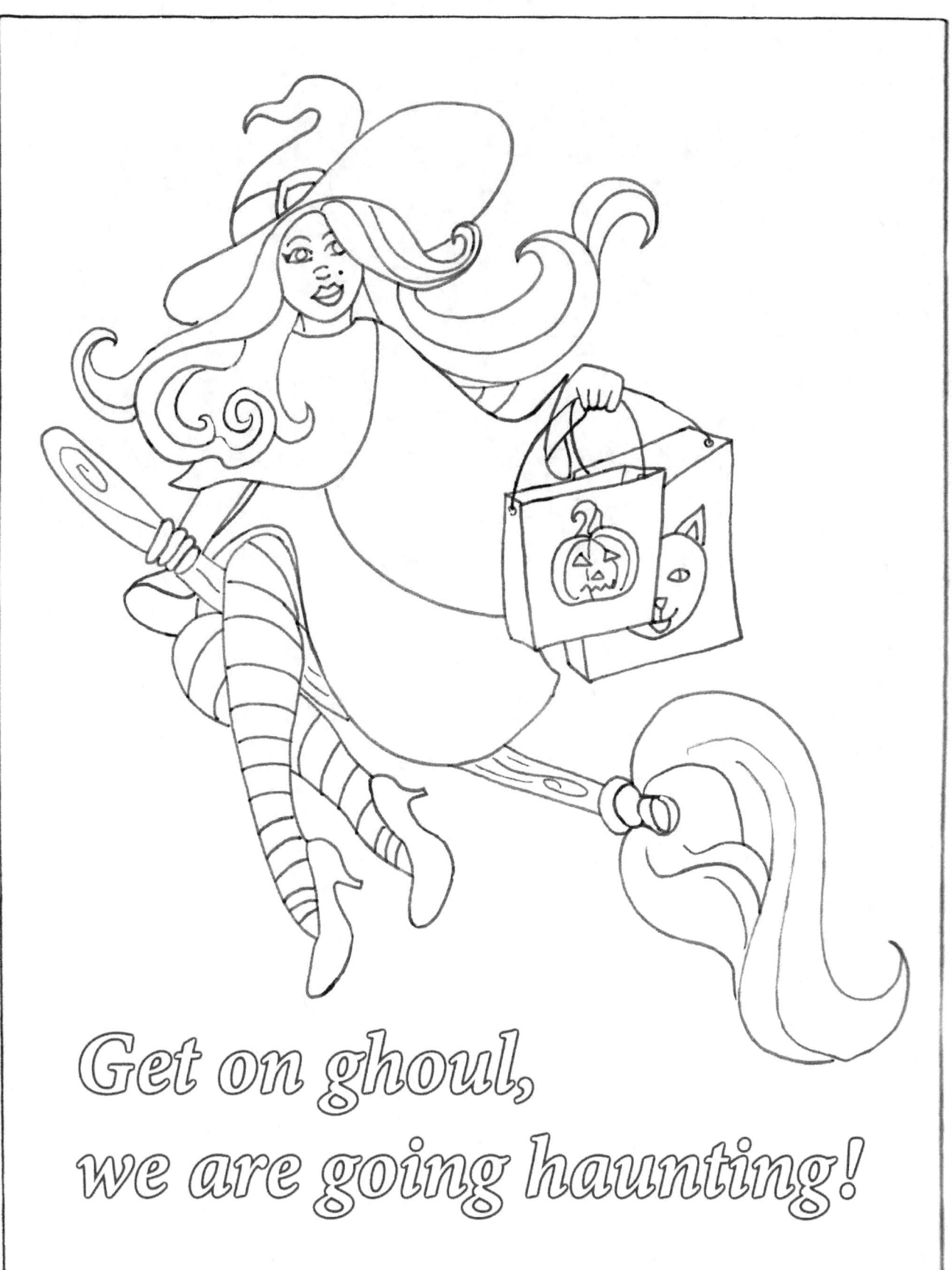

Get on ghoul,
we are going haunting!

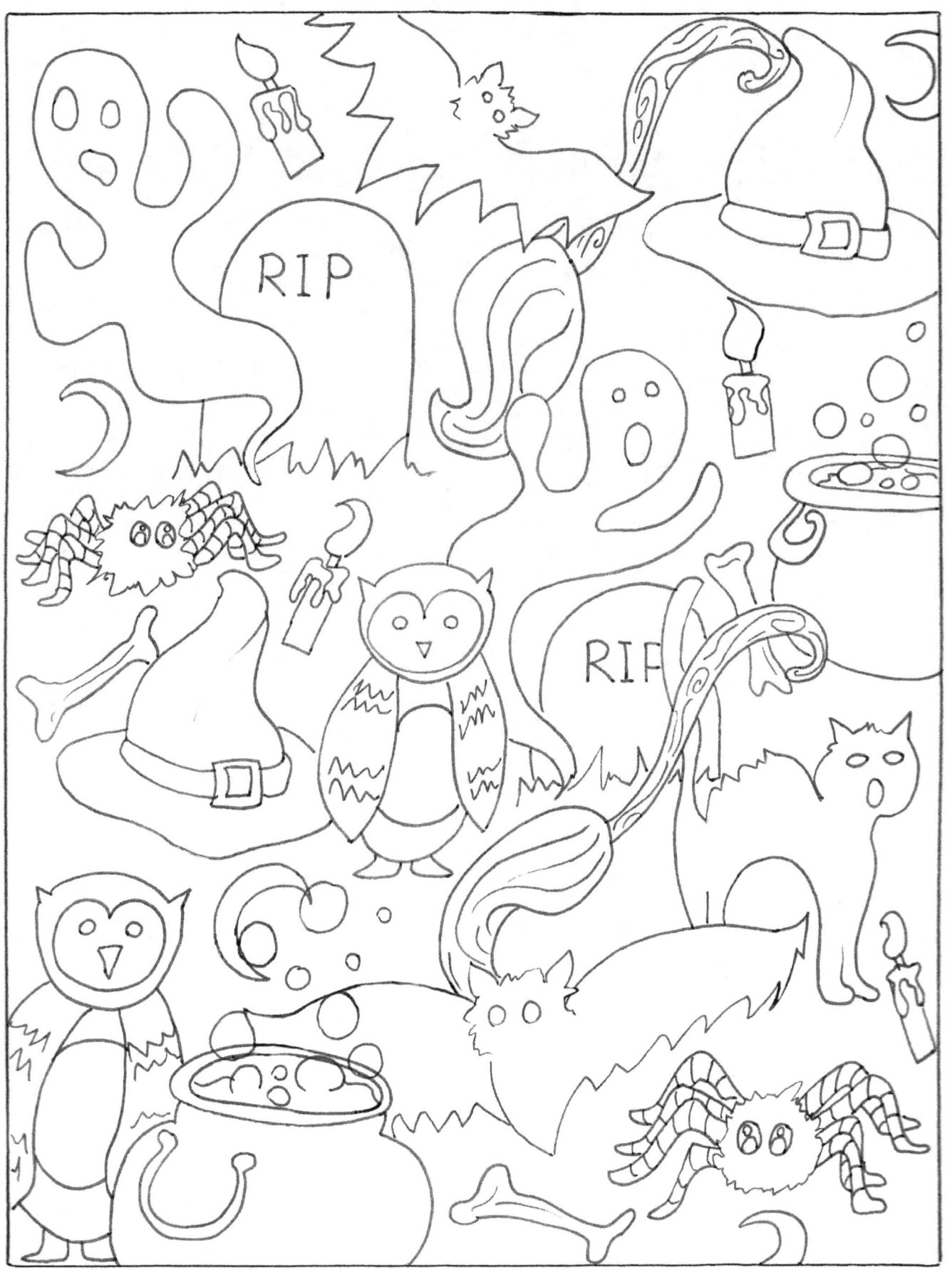

If you got it....

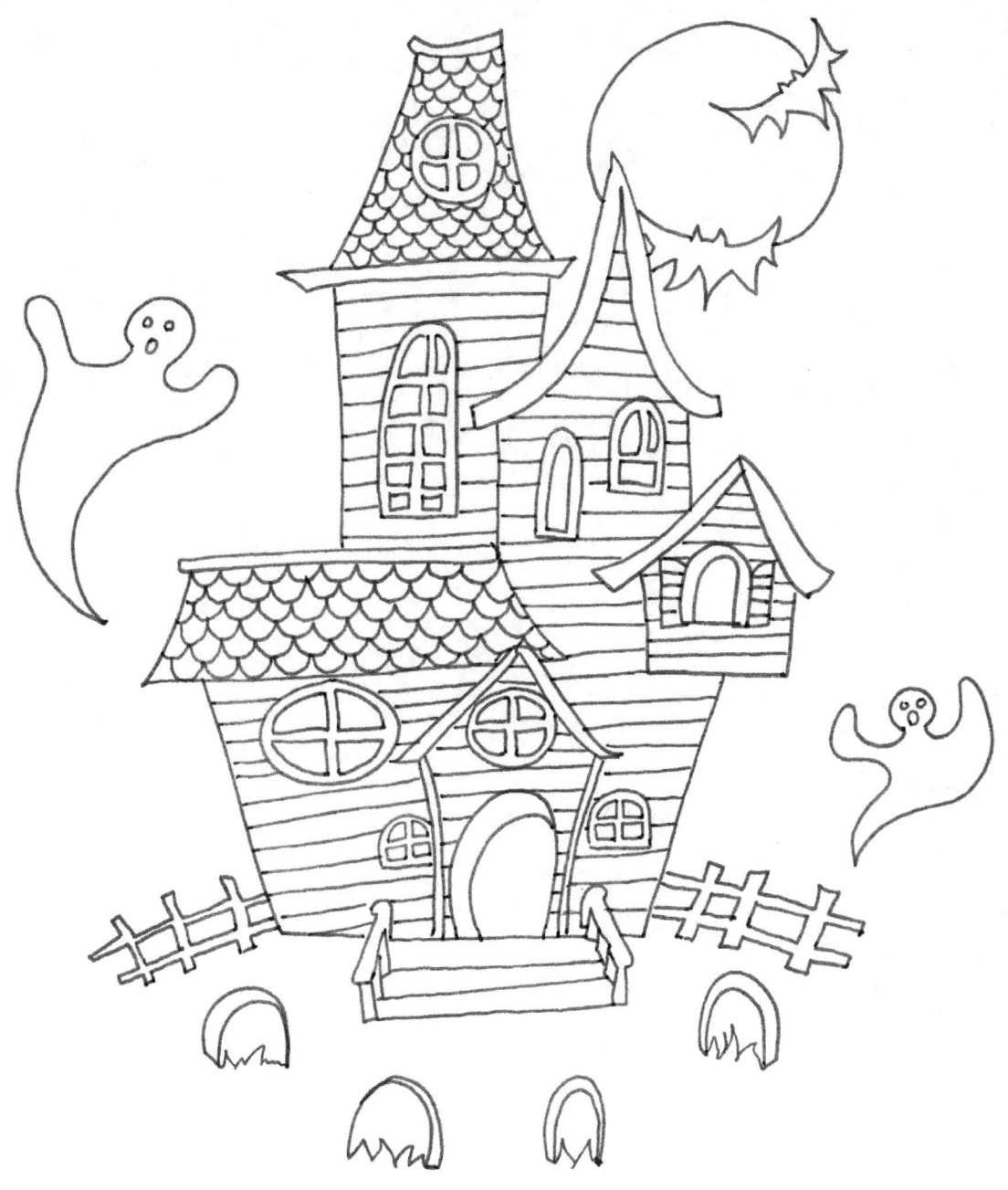

Haunt it!

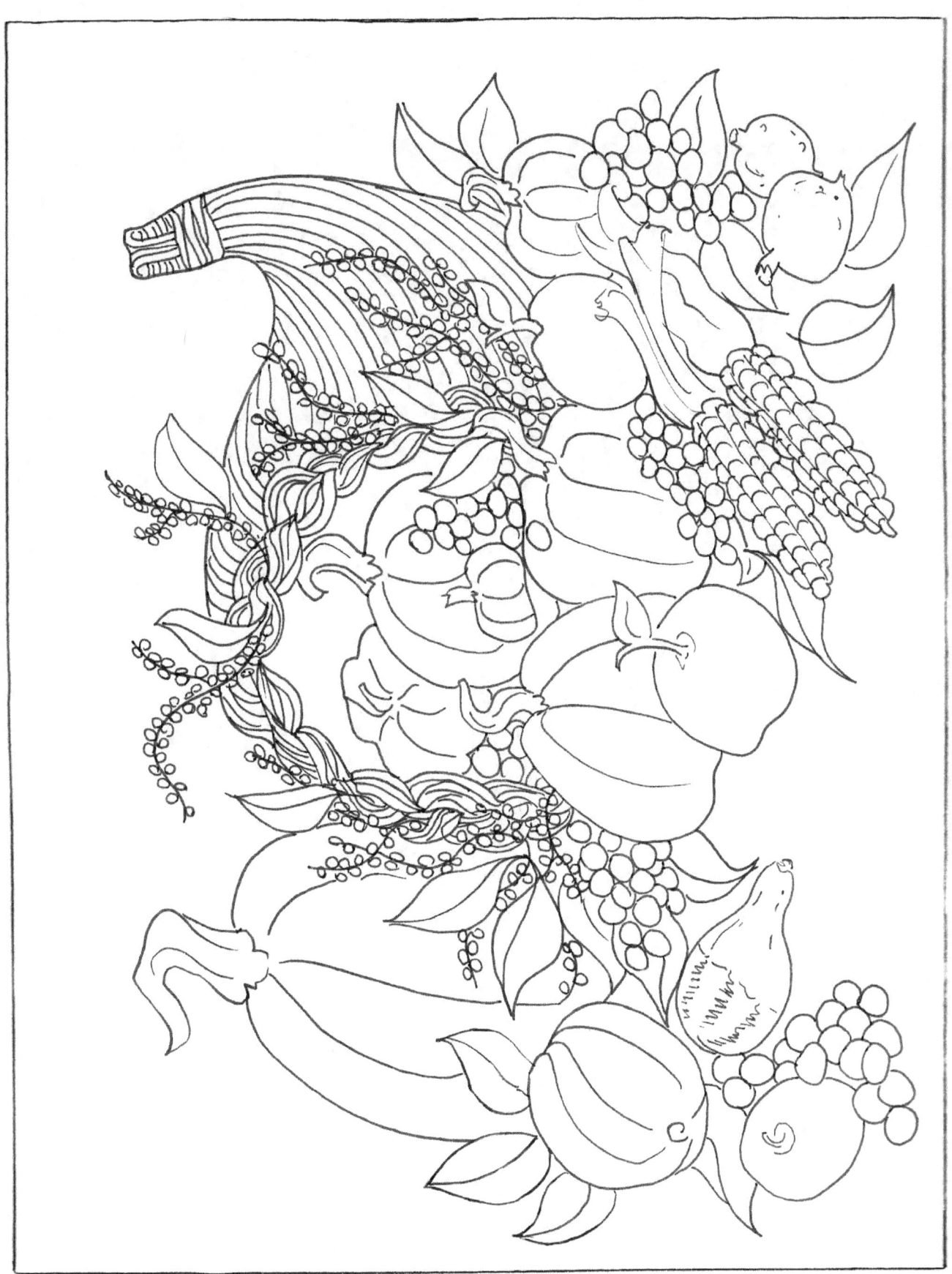

FARMERS MARKET

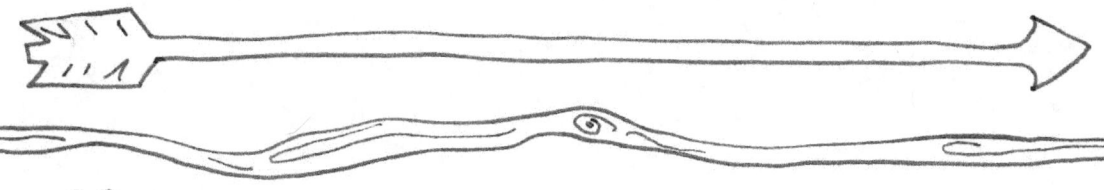

Fresh Cut Flowers

PUMPKIN PATCH

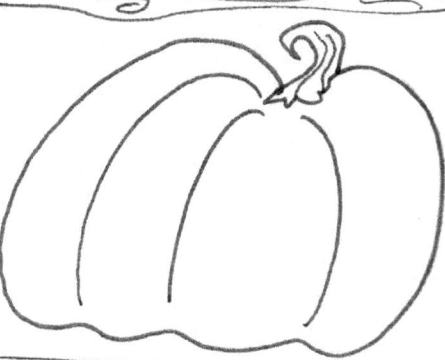

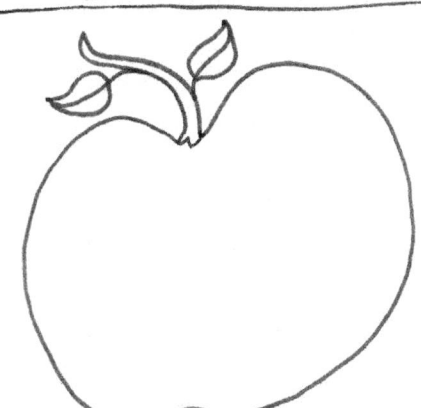

Apple Picking

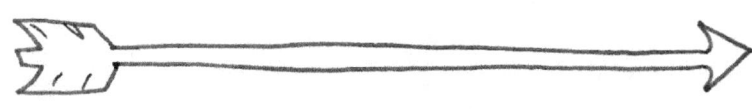

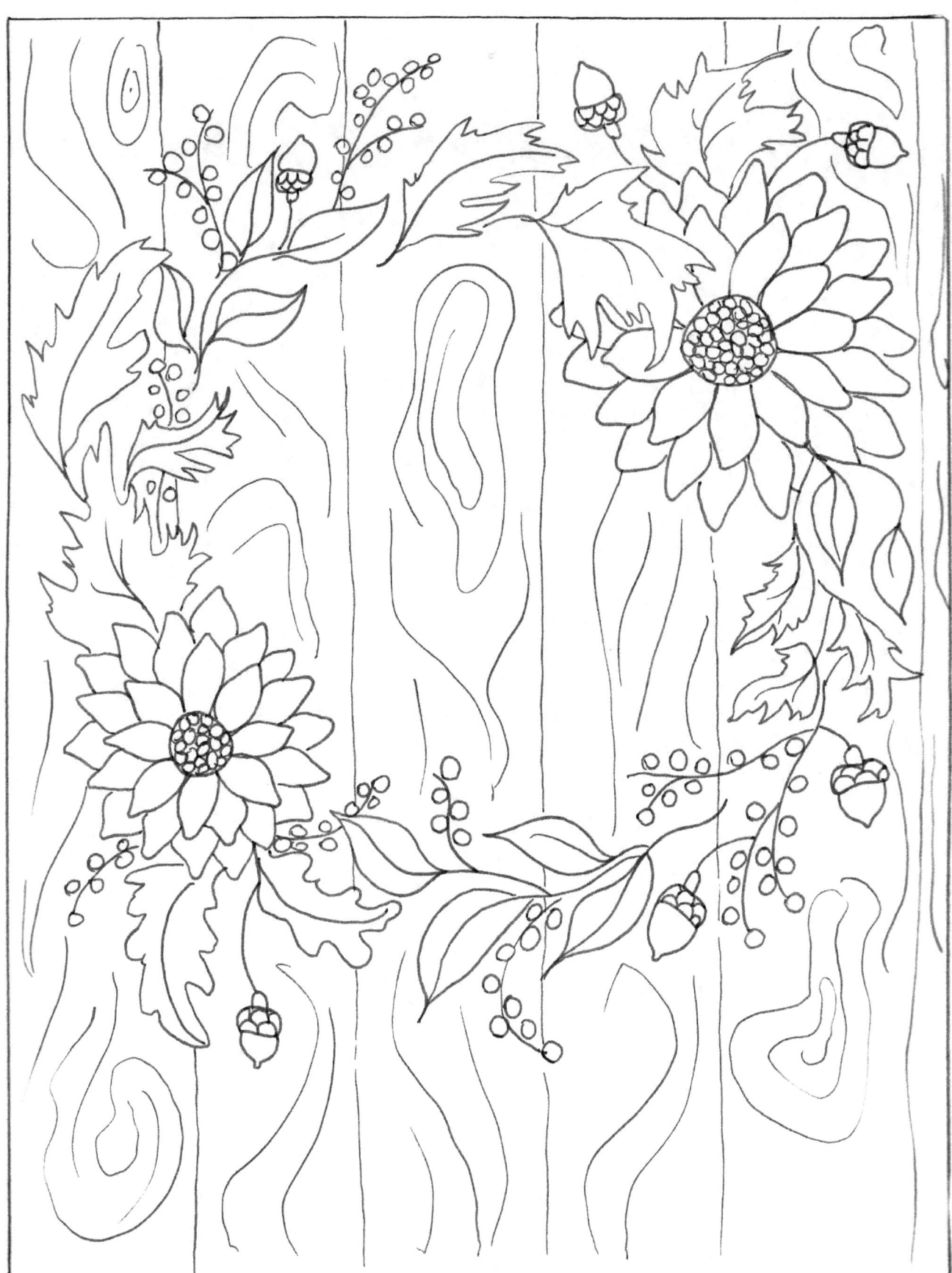

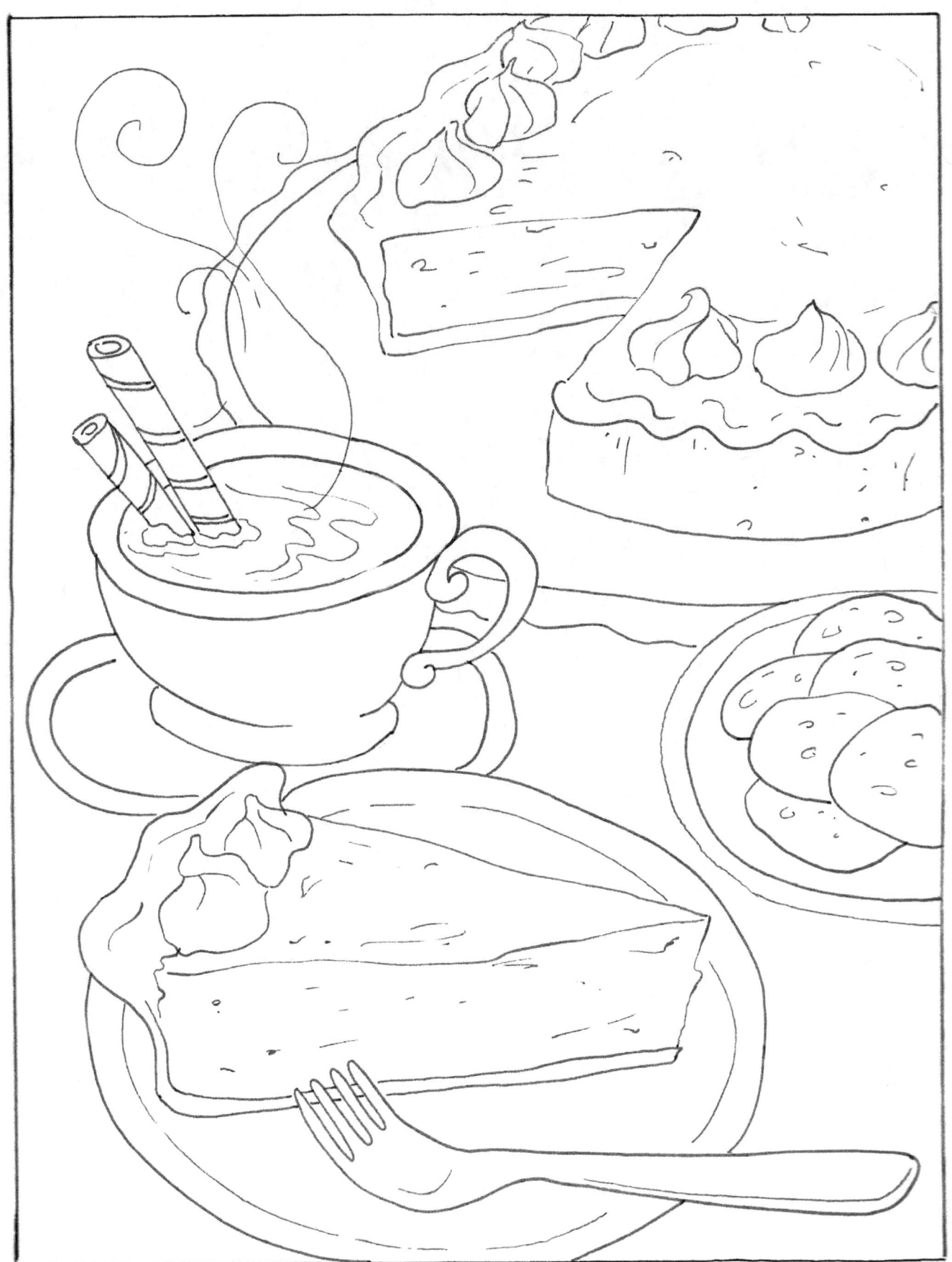

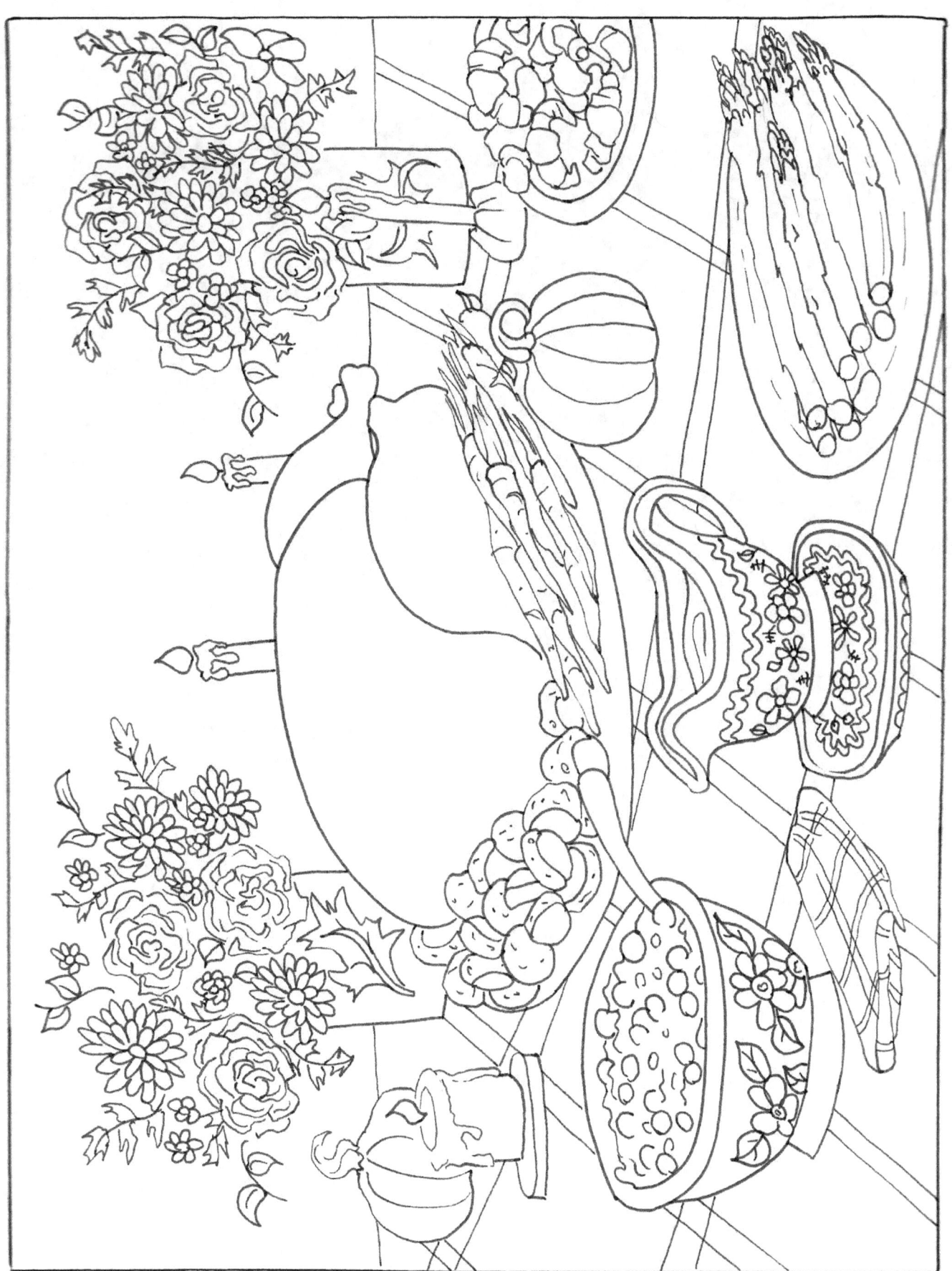

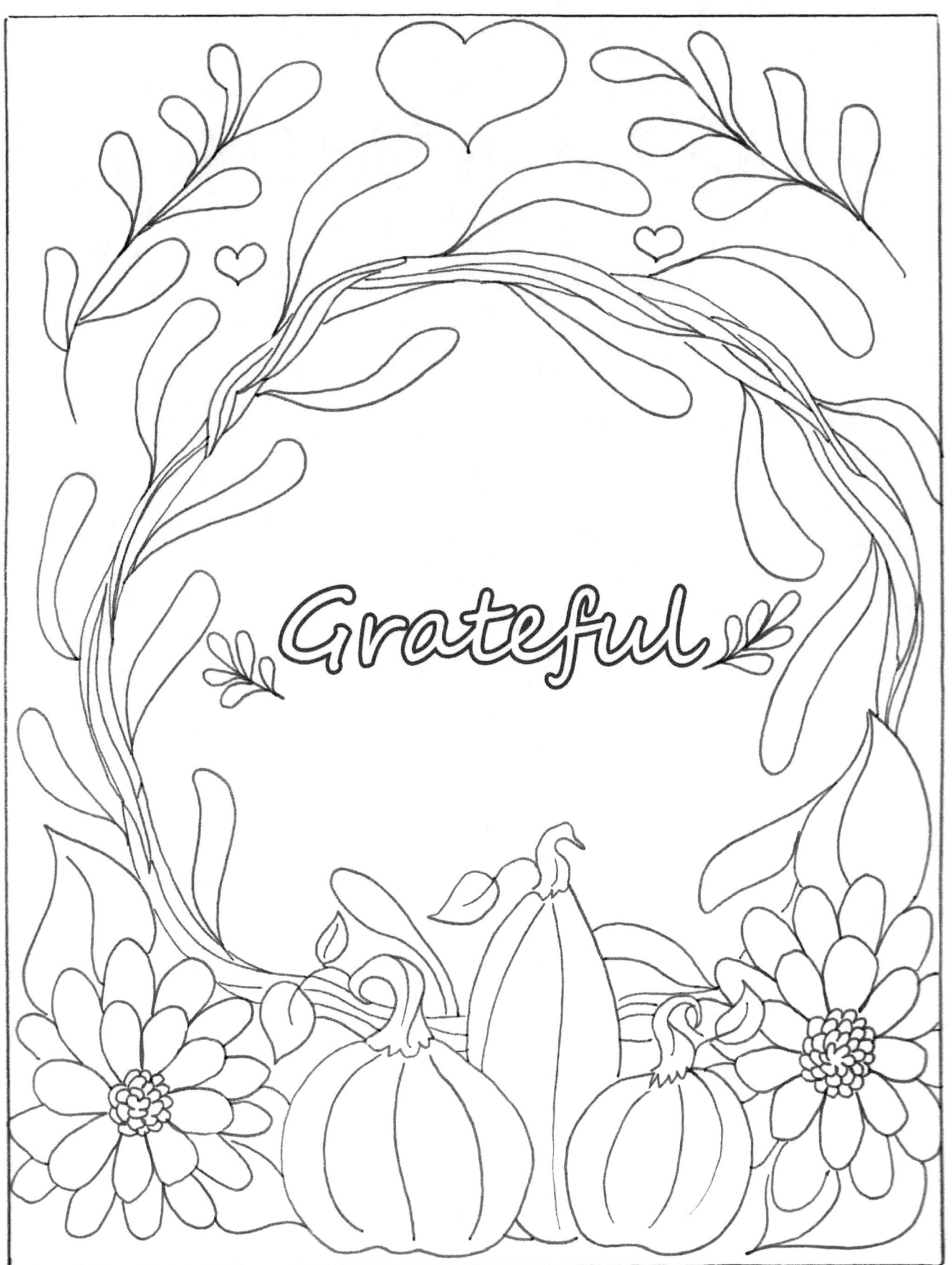

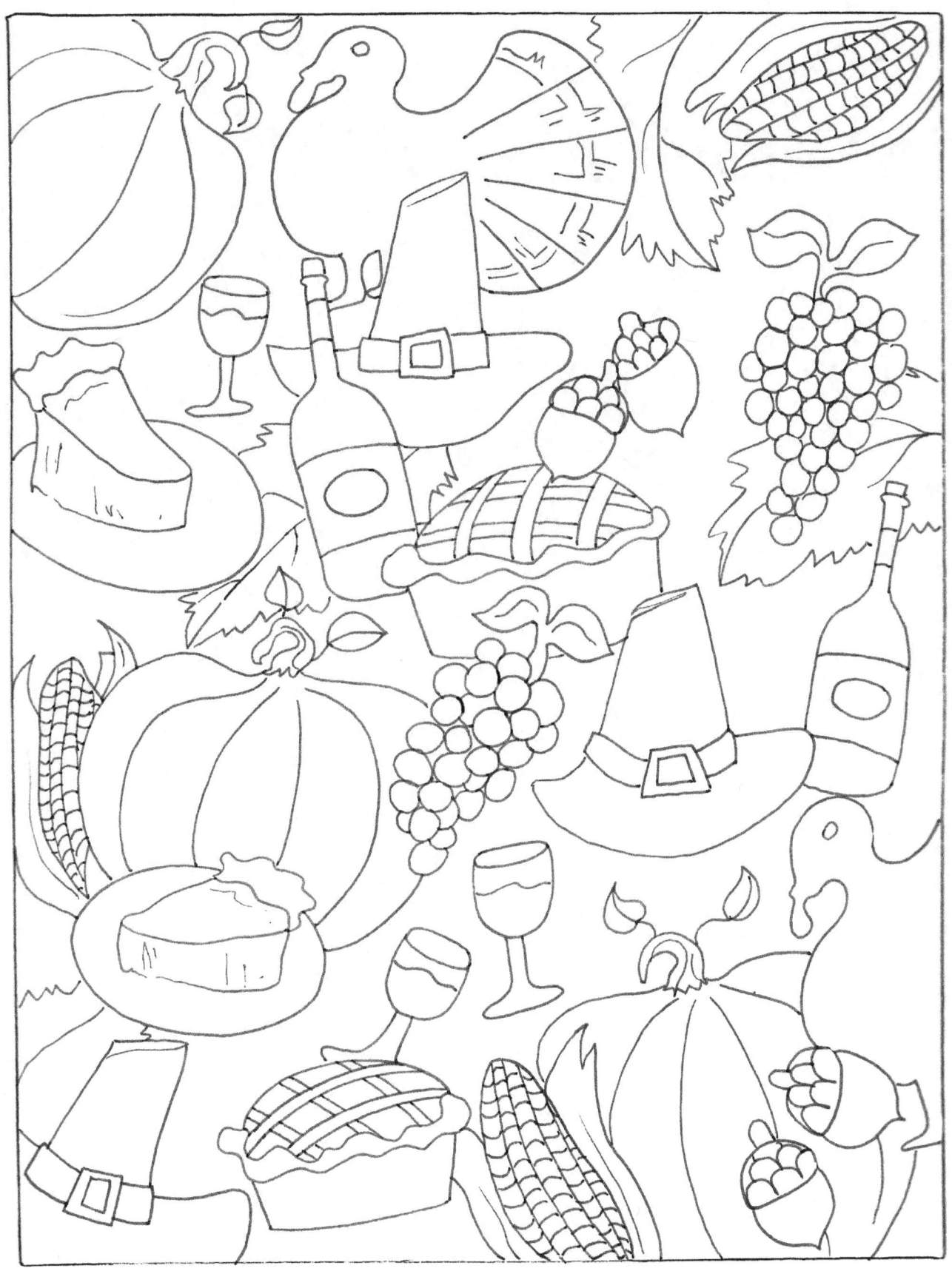

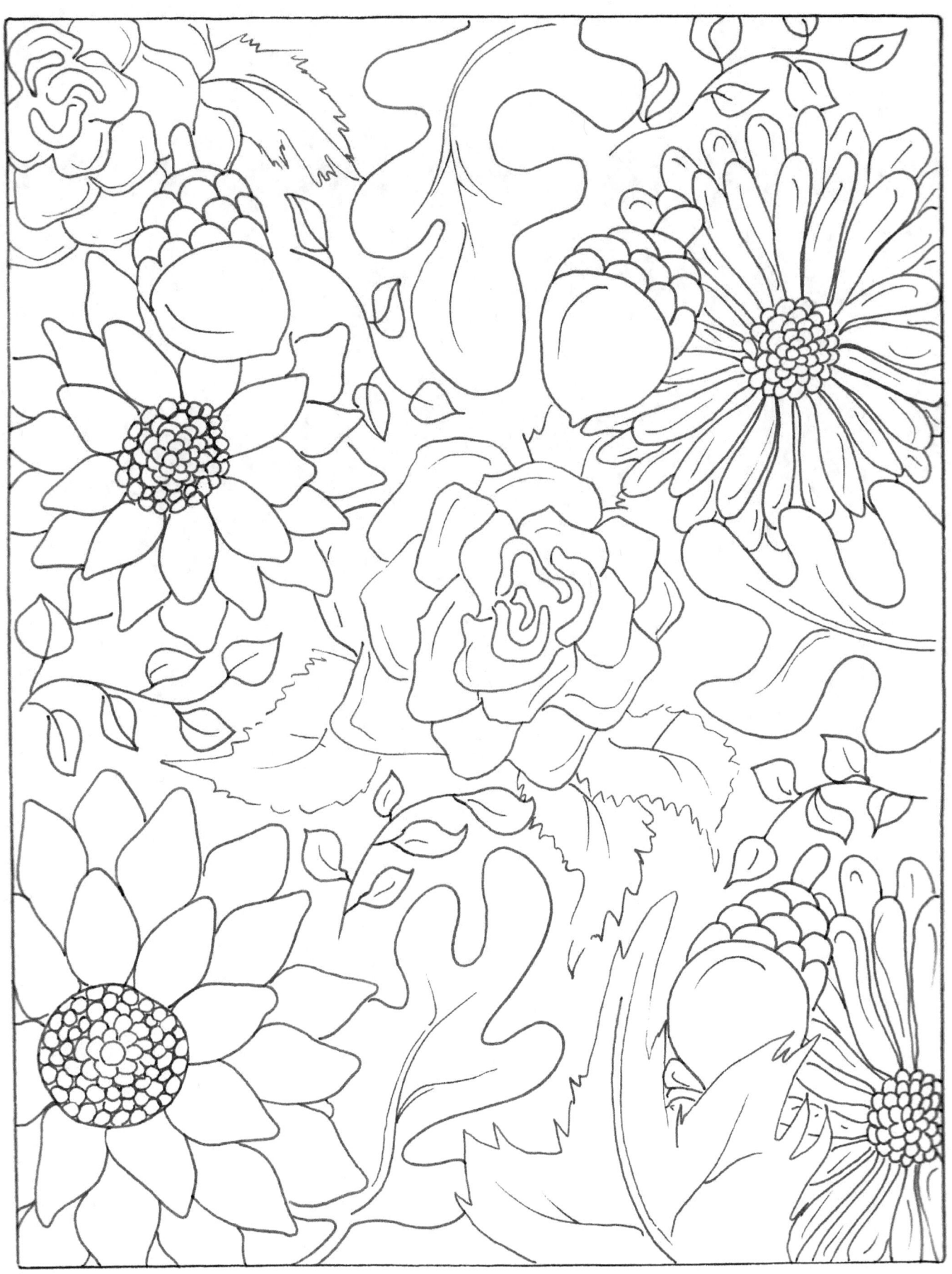